TACOMA

TACOMA

Photography by Cindy McIntyre

Text by Denny MacGougan

Produced by Richard C. Anderson

Design by Mitzi Tallman McCart
Typography by R-4 Typographers, Inc. • Tacoma
Copyright© MCMLXXXVIII by Baker/Anderson Enterprises • Fox Island, Washington
All rights reserved
Published by Baker/Anderson Enterprises
Printed by Graphic Arts Center • Portland, Oregon U.S.A.

ISBN 0-9621335-0-7
Library of Congress Catalog Number 88-092269

From Old Town, where just about everybody has a view. That's Brown's Point to the north, with the lighthouse just visible in the marinescape background.

Overleaf: The blue of an evening sits well in this view of downtown, an imaginary reflection perhaps, from the multi-shades of blue from the roof of the city's famous domed stadium.

Neighborhoods mirror the livability of a city, and in Tacoma there is a neighborhood for everyone. Virtually all make the visual statement, "it's a great place to live."

Growing Up In Tacoma

When I was a little girl, growing up in Tacoma, I couldn't imagine how anyone could live anywhere else in the United States, or the world for that matter.

I was born in Tacoma and have lived in this city most of my life.

Except for a brief time during World War II when my father was in the Army, during college and a few years as a military wife, I have always lived in Tacoma and I love this city.

When I was about a year old, my father built a colonial-style house on North Tacoma Avenue where my family lived for more than 20 years. For many of those years, there was a vacant lot across the street which was one of my favorite places to play. Our house also was close to the Tacoma Lawn Tennis Club where I learned to play tennis and later learned synchronized swimming. When I was in high school I played tennis as a member of the Junior Wightman Cup team. My son learned to play tennis at TLTC.

One of my earlier recollections of growing up in Tacoma was the terrific blizzard we had in 1950. On the first day of the blizzard, January 13, my mother decided to take my sister and me along with her when she went to take care of some business at the old court house on Eleventh Street. She parked the car on the hill, left us in the car and started across the street in the howling wind and blowing snow. She literally blew across the street and my sister and I were sure we would never see her again. Of course we did.

That blizzard lasted for days and forced all schools in the city to be closed. That was the best part about it but the snow drifts were so

Larry Anderson's bronze sculptures have become a joyful segment of Tacoma's art scene. This one, entitled "Trilogy," is in Wright Park.

high and the wind blew so fiercely that we couldn't go out and play in it for several days. Every time our little cocker spaniel had to go outside we were sure he would get lost in a snow drift.

When we finally could go out and play in the snow, we had some great sledding on G Street. Someone who lived nearby had a huge toboggan which held several people. What fun that was!

We had more snow when I was growing up than we do now. When I was a little older, I discovered the delights of sledding or inner-tubing in the snow on Carr Street. It was a wonderful ride down, almost all the way to Commencement Bay, but it was a long way back up.

My school years were all spent at the Annie Wright School which was just two and a half blocks from our house. I began at Annie Wright (then called Annie Wright Seminary) in a three-year kindergarten and graduated from high school in 1957. Each year when I was in high school I begged my parents to let me go to Stadium High School and they'd let me think I would go there — until classes started again at Annie Wright. (Incidentally, both my son and daughter graduated from Stadium.)

The school year at Annie Wright began with one of many of the school's traditions, Annie's Birthday Party. That was our first opportunity to meet the new students and renew old acquaintances. At the same time the seniors began hunting for the spade which had been hidden by the previous graduating class. The spade was used at the end of the school year, by the seniors, to plant a tree somewhere on the school grounds. A second tradition was the Christmas Carol service in the chapel, with all the students dressed in white and wearing white veils. The same was true of the Easter Carol service. Another favorite tradition was May Day, with the May Queen being elected from the senior class. At that time, the entire student body, dressed in white, took part in the May Day procession and later danced for the queen and her court which consisted of the rest of the senior class. One of the dances was always the May Pole dance which prevails today.

Finally, the traditions surrounding graduation were probably my favorite. There was always an alumnae luncheon where the seniors were introduced, the first determined by the number of years she had attended the school. There were two of us who had been there for 13 years. It was also announced where each senior would be attending college. During graduation weekend the seniors read their will, planted a tree, gave a gift to the school, were honored at a baccalaureate service and the graduation ceremony included presentation of the many

One of our jewels, at Point Defiance Park.

awards — from art to scholarship and citizenship. Another of the traditions during graduation weekend was called "step singing," at which time the juniors sang songs they had written, while standing on senior stairs. That signaled the official use by the juniors of that set of stairs, in the front hall of the school.

Another of my early recollections is a sad one. We had a powerful earthquake when I was still in grade school. The date of the earthquake was April 13, 1949. The impact of the earthquake caused one of the brick towers at Lowell Elementary School to crumble and one of my neighbors, who was a member of the school patrol, was killed by a shower of bricks after he had pushed a younger boy to safety.

One of my favorite things to do when I was growing up in Tacoma was riding bikes in our neighborhood and all through Petrich Point. One of my friends and I occasionally rode our bikes along Ruston Way, through Ruston to Point Defiance Park. While in the park we always visited Dub Dub, Tacoma's favorite harbor seal who died some years ago. There is now a bronze statue of Dub Dub, by Larry Anderson, by the tidal pool exhibit at the aquarium. Of course, then the zoo was nowhere near the world class zoo that Tacoma has now, but it was still a favorite place to spend a lazy, summer afternoon.

Interestingly, my fondness for the zoo was enhanced during my career at The Tacoma News Tribune in the 1980s. As a reporter for three years, part of my responsibility was covering the parks, in particular the renovation of the zoo. I followed the renovation process from beginning to end with stories almost weekly. A favorite memory of that time was when E.T. Walrus was rescued and I was sent to Anchorage, Alaska to meet some of the zoo staff and fly with him to Tacoma. I still consider E.T. to be a good friend.

My career at the Tribune actually started in the summer of 1958 after my freshman year in college at Colby Sawyer College in New London, New Hampshire. I was hired as a reporter and wrote everything from obits to weddings and occasional feature stories. It was a real learning experience which continued each summer of my college years, the latter two at the University of Washington. At that time, my grandfather, Frank S. Baker, was publisher of the newspaper but I hardly ever saw him at work. I think he preferred to keep his family on the staff low key. After his death in 1961, my father, Elbert H. Baker II became publisher.

Following my summer experiences, my career at the Tribune didn't resume until 1976 when I was hired to work in the Credit Department. After nine months, I was loaned to United Way for three months as a Loaned Executive during the fall campaign. I'm still active in United Way, as a member of the board and a campaign volunteer. Upon returning to the Tribune I worked for the Personnel Department, then the newsroom, and finally back to Personnel until I left the Tribune when it was sold in 1986 to the McClatchy family of California. At that time the newspaper had been in my family for 73 years.

Some of the special times when I was growing up were during family parties and reunions. Each Thanksgiving our family celebrated at one of my aunt's houses. The adults all ate upstairs in the big dining room while the kids and grandchildren ate together downstairs in the recreation room. For several years at Christmas time, we had a family tree-cutting party in Bangor at the Navy base near Silverdale where my uncle was commanding officer. We all went out in the woods, often in the snow, and cut down our own Christmas tree and then came back to warm up in front of the huge fireplace before having a great family dinner. Finally, we always had a family party on my grandfather's birthday, July 27. We all swam in the lake in front of his house on American Lake, played badminton and had a great spaghetti dinner that Grandpa had cooked.

The neighborhood I grew up in was an interesting one. Just down the hill was the old Saint Peter's Church, the first church in the city. Somewhere down another hill was a rock with a plaque on it stating that it was where Job Carr had first settled. It was a neighborhood of diverse people, with a large group of neighbors being Slavonian fishermen. It was a neighborhood better known now as Old Town.

One of my fondest memories is of riding horses through the horse trails at Point Defiance Park. One of my cousins owned a horse which she kept in the large stable at the park. My sister and I used to go riding with her once a week; it was always exhilarating. I had one mishap that I can recall, when the horse I was riding threw me off after being frightened by

Obviously a home, not just a house.

something on the trail. I cracked my collarbone and was taped up for sometime after that. Later, when I was in college, I learned that a fire had destroyed the stable and there has been no horseback riding in the park since.

I used to ice skate, too, when I was younger. We often went to the Lakewood Ice Arena on Saturdays and skated for hours. It was a very popular place. On September 25, 1974 the fire marshal closed the arena because of fire hazards and unsafe conditions and demolition of the building took place in 1982.

When I was little, downtown Tacoma was bustling with retail shops and lots of shoppers. There was Rhodes and The Bon Marche, Sears, J.C. Penneys and the People's Store. There was also Gundersons, Frasers and Lou Johnsons. Whenever we went downtown, our mother made us dress up and we never saw people shopping who were dressed in jeans the way they do now. Downtown changed dramatically when the Tacoma Mall was built and gradually all of the stores moved out there. Today there are some very fine specialty shops, including antique shops, in downtown Tacoma and toward the close of 1988, plans were for more stores to return. In addition, downtown Tacoma boasts numerous banks, businesses and the University of Puget Sound Law School. Thanks to Cornerstone Columbia Development Company many of the older buildings have been renovated and new buildings have been built. The newest, the Frank Russell Company building, adds a handsome dimension to Tacoma's skyline and the proposed plans for the historic Union Station are encouraging.

My love affair with Tacoma continues to this day. From my office in the Tacoma Financial Center, I can watch the ships come into the Port of Tacoma, a sign that the City of Destiny is thriving in an exciting way. Tacoma has been good to me, and with this book, I hope to be able to give something back to this community which has nurtured me since the day I was born.

Martine Baker

This landmark hamburger joint was destroyed by fire, was rebuilt, and the only complaint about the new operation was that the 'burgers weren't greasy enough.

Overleaf: In this "says it all" view of downtown from the City Waterway, the facade of the spanking new (1988) Frank Russell Company building unequivocably states: "We like it here!"

'My kind of town, Tacoma is'

By Denny MacGougan

That line originally was written for a song about Chicago. I have been to Chicago and, frankly, Chicago is not my kind of town. Tacoma is.

So I have stolen the line. A petty theft, really, one that Chicago — nurtured in the traditions of Al Capone and Mayor Richard Daley — probably won't even notice. Tacoma, on the other hand, has been the victim of some really grand larceny. The Mountain, for instance. Seattle interests successfully foiled several major Tacoma efforts to restore Mount Rainier's original Indian name, Mount Tacoma.

Tacoma is a little like a beautiful woman who is accident-prone. Most of us who live here remain smitten, devoted admirers and defenders, ruefully shaking our heads at the gaffes and pratfalls. And, though few admit it, I suspect that most Tacomans are secretly pleased that Tacoma has never been a major success. Then we'd have had to share.

In springtime, an umbrella is all you need when showers fall — especially if you're with the right person.

A lot of the attraction, for me, lies just above my typewriter. I have the good fortune to live and work on a bluff in Tacoma's North End, overlooking Commencement Bay. My vista includes a good portion of the magnificent deep-water harbor, backed by the green Northeast Tacoma hillside, with Vashon Island and the distant, snow-capped Olympics off to the Northwest.

To my right, a couple of ocean-going Foss tugs are guiding a large, orange containership through a swarm of small sailboats toward the Port of Tacoma piers. To my left, one of the city's two lime-yellow hovercraft fireboats speeds along toward some important mission — probably lunch.

The Northeast Tacoma hillside tapers down toward the West to end at Browns Point, where I can see the sun glinting off the small lighthouse and its tall flagpole. It was around Browns Point that British Capt. George Vancouver was rowed by some crewmen on a May evening in 1792.

Confronting for the first time the vista which subsequent settlers have come to cherish, Vancouver was understandably impressed with the fortuitous marriage of water, forest and mountain. He had first spotted the majestic, volcanic peak from the northern reaches of Puget Sound and had named it for his friend, English Adm. Peter Rainier. It was a gesture which would provoke a bitter long-running feud between Seattle and Tacoma over the name.

Vancouver wrote in his journal of The Mountain's "perpetual clothing of snow" and the "most grand, picturesque effect" produced by the scene. I suspect he also was thinking: "Pete, you owe me one!" The admiral certainly did.

Forty-nine years later the first American expedition, led by Navy Lt. Charles Wilkes, anchored below my bluff to begin charting southern Puget Sound. Wilkes named the bay, appropriately, "Commencement."

Flattering descriptions of the unspoiled Puget Sound area began appearing in the East, and settlers started trickling in. Olympia got a few, Steilacoom got a few, and Tacoma was about to get a few when gold was discovered in California. Most of the Northwest-bound adventurers turned left and became "Forty-Niners."

One who resisted the temptation was a young Swede named Nick Delin. He could see

Growth of Port of Tacoma's operations in the 1980's has been phenomenal. Ships bearing general cargo containers, automobiles and timber come and go daily.

the promise of gold in the forests of tall trees which lined the shores of Puget Sound. Delin was able to borrow enough money in Olympia to set up a sawmill on a creek at the head of Commencement Bay. He built himself a home, added some cabins for workmen, and by late 1852, his water-powered muley saw was cutting 2,000 feet of lumber (on days when the saw didn't hang up too often).

The next year, the first overland wagon train reached the bay. It was led by James Longmire and utilized Naches Pass in the tough trek across the Cascades.

Eleven years later, Job Carr, a discharged Union veteran who'd heard that a transcontinental railroad was due to terminate hereabouts, made it to Olympia. Out fishing near Gig Harbor in a canoe owned by some new-found friends, they decided to paddle along the bay's south shore. Suddenly, Carr stood up in the canoe (somehow escaping a dunking) and shouted "Eureka! Eureka!"

Carr had spotted a gentle draw in the otherwise high-bank waterfront and it was love at first sight.

A successful downtown rejuvenation project, Court C Market is connected to Broadway Plaza, between 11th and 13th.

There, Carr built a home, summoned his relatives from the East, and with subsequent arrivals, such as Matthew McCarver and Clinton Ferry, founded what would become Old Tacoma. Actually, what would become New Tacoma, near Delin's millsite, was older than Old Tacoma, but those were Troubled Times.

Old and New Tacomas eventually merged in 1884, quit squabbling so much with each other, and tried to take on a common enemy, Seattle. Prospects for the two major cities on the Sound appeared fairly even at the time, and a betting man might have put money on Tacoma.

But there were those pratfalls yet to come.

For some 35 years, much of the local civic energy went into the campaign to get "Tacoma" recognized as the official name for The Mountain. There was considerable evidence and a whole lot of local sentiment for the proposition that the resident Indians had called the peak "Tacoma" or a variation thereof, most notably "Tahoma."

From 1883, all mountain references in the local press read "Mount Tacoma," boosters interviewed agreeable Puyallups and Nisquallys, and a drive was begun to get the name changed officially on the nation's maps. But if Tacoma was for it, Seattle was against it.

Despite support for the Indian name from President Theodore Roosevelt, the Smithsonian Institution and the Northern Pacific Railroad (which had selected New Tacoma as its Western terminus and was busy selling lots) Seattle's clout was to beat back three impressively mounted "Mount Tacoma" pitches before the U.S. Board of Geographic Names.

When Tacomans finally took their case directly to Congress in 1924, U.S. Sen. Clarence Dill of Spokane managed to get a "Mount Tacoma" resolution passed unanimously by a voice vote in the Senate. Victory finally seemed attainable in the long fight, but the Seattle forces rallied and managed to keep the resolution bottled up in a House committee until Congress adjourned.

In 1925, the Tacoma Chamber of Commerce threw in the towel.

Tacoma had been outmuscled in the Tacoma-Rainier fight, but was simply outhustled in the days following the 1896 discovery of gold on the Yukon River in Alaska. Seattle immediately hired a publicity man and

*Snaking into Commencement Bay is the Puyallup
River; the larger bridge carries traffic on Interstate 5.*

sent him East to trumpet the boast that Seattle — and only Seattle — was the Gateway to Alaska.

In Tacoma, which had been harder hit by the financial Panic of 1893, city officials were embroiled in a donnybrook over some election results. A recount was proving difficult since the locked ballot boxes had been stolen from the city vault.

Then there was the first Narrows Bridge, which was to make quite a splash. Long efforts by local politicians to get the state to build a suspension bridge across the Narrows, linking Tacoma with the growing Kitsap Peninsula, finally saw the span open in 1940.

The bridge, nicknamed "Galloping Gertie," was to collapse on Nov. 7, 1940, just four months after it had opened. The day was especially dark for a local insurance agent who had sold the state much of the insurance on the bridge and had simply pocketed the premiums. What could ever happen to a multi-million dollar bridge? The insurance company eventually made good on the claim, while its agent spent some time behind bars.

Of the many Larry Anderson sculptures in Tacoma, this one in front of the historic Union Station is probably seen the most frequently.

In 1951, Tacoma's dirty linen was aired on television as State Sen. Al Rosellini brought his Senate Crime Committee hearings to Tacoma. The hearings made celebrities of some Tacoma madams, like Amanda Truelove, buffoons of Tacoma officials, and ultimately a two-term governor of Rosellini.

Tacoma's luck was typified by Lt. Harold Bromley's projected, history-making 1929 flight to Japan in the sturdy monoplane "Spirit of Tacoma," an effort financed by local sponsors and hundreds of small contributions. It would be the first non-stop flight to the Orient and was front-page news in Tacoma for months. The dashing Bromley made dozens of fund-raising talks before local civic groups, each providing him with a plaque or memento for the Japanese emperor.

On the day of Bromley's scheduled departure, thousands of cheering, flag-waving Tacomans lined the runway of the old Pierce County Airport, now part of the McChord Air Force Base complex.

Loaded down with fuel and plaques, poor Bromley's airplane never was able to get off the ground. On the second try, the plane crashed at the end of the runway, and Bromley narrowly escaped with his life.

Tacoma's fortunes have been on a definite upswing since the late '70s. It would appear the old girl finally has learned to keep her balance.

The big orange ship crossing my windowpane is part of a parade which has seen Tacoma's port business grow to virtually equal Seattle's. The local port has even stolen a few major customers from the city to the north.

Downtown Tacoma has seen a major revitalization and substantial new construction. The Cornerstone Co., a development arm of the Weyerhaeuser Co., was instrumental in getting an award-winning Sheraton Hotel and neighboring Financial Center built and opened, while the Tacoma-based Frank Russell Co. in 1988 completed a handsome new high-rise headquarters building on a downtown bluff.

Voters indebted themselves to erect the Tacoma Dome, a 25,000-seat all-wood arena (a first) near the Interstate 5 Freeway. The Dome has lured entertainment superstars such as Frank Sinatra and Bruce Springsteen;

Mt. Rainier reflected in a still, alpine lake during the summer season.

major sporting events like the 1987 National Figure Skating Championships; and has served as home for the Tacoma Stars franchise in the Major Indoor Soccer League.

Tacoma's Triple-A Tigers, playing in Cheney Stadium, considered one of the nation's finest minor league baseball parks, occasionally outdraw the Seattle Mariners, playing big-league ball in the Kingdome, on sunny afternoons.

The Western Washington Fair, a September staple in neighboring Puyallup, has become one of the nation's biggest, luring the likes of Bob Hope, Red Skelton and Willie Nelson.

Tacoma's two private universities, the University of Puget Sound and Pacific Lutheran University, continue to grow in enrollment and prestige. The city's military neighbors, Fort Lewis and McChord AFB, keep receiving added responsibilities for the nation's defense.

Meanwhile, the second Narrows Bridge continues to stand, and Seattle never has figured out how to steal Point Defiance Park.

There may be a message here for Lt. Harold Bromley, wherever he is:

It looks like the Spirit of Tacoma is finally off the ground!

*Still perking along is this art deco fixture on South
Tacoma Way — the Java Jive.*

*Overleaf: There are simply not enough superlatives to
describe the majesty of Tacoma's mountain, called
Rainier. This is Cindy McIntyre's most recent image.*

Commencement Bay provides year 'round boating, but in the spring and fall, spinnaker-rigged sailboats display colors on a regular schedule of yacht club competitions.

Spic 'n span, these boats await the commercial fishing season opening. Moored across the Narrows Bridge in the tranquil waters of Tacoma's neighbor, Gig Harbor, the boats represent an historical industry of Puget Sound.

These are homes in the unique neighborhood community of Salmon Beach, on the Narrows just south of the bridge. Accessible only on foot.

Individual preference for architectural design is the mark of Salmon Beach residents.

Overleaf: Looking north from downtown, to Brown's Point (foreground) and Dash Point, two burgeoning residential areas fronting Commencement Bay and Puget Sound.

The Setting

To fully appreciate Tacoma's ambiance, a little altitude adjustment helps. And if you lack access to a helicopter or a hot air balloon, imagination will have to do. Imagine you are a pigeon — heck, be an eagle if you want to — perched atop the spire of the First Presbyterian Church at Division and Tacoma Avenues.

Looking north, Commencement Bay, one of the world's great deep-water harbors, is spread out before you. In the background is the Northeast Tacoma hillside, with the sprawling Federal Way area beyond. Skirting Browns Point, the great ships head north up East Passage, passing Vashon/Maury Island on the left and the communities of Dash Point, Redondo, Des Moines and Burien on the right as they head for Seattle's Elliott Bay, the Strait of Juan de Fuca and the Pacific Ocean. On a clear day, you can see downtown Seattle's 76-story Columbia Center tower, not to mention Mount Baker, near Bellingham.

As you swivel your feathered head to the west, the

Heading for Talequah on Vashon Island is a regularly scheduled Washington State ferry.

city's stately residential North End marches out to Point Defiance and its magnificent park, with Gig Harbor and the Olympic Mountains beyond. Due west the Sound funnels into the Narrows, spanned by the second Narrows Bridge, gateway to the Longbranch, Kitsap and Olympic Peninsulas. As the rotation continues the foreground produces Day Island, University Place and Steilacoom; the background Fox, McNeil, Anderson and Hartstene Islands, rich with waterways and wooded homesites.

Now you are looking south, toward Tacoma's Lakes District, where American, Steilacoom and Gravelly Lakes once were the sites of summer homes for local timber barons and picnic grounds for less affluent city streetcar riders. Now the lakes are ringed with beautiful, year-around homes, with residential and commercial developments having taken over most of the surrounding prairie. Beyond the lakes to the south are two of the nation's major military installations, Fort Lewis and McChord Air Force Base, augmented by Madigan Army Hospital, American Lake Veterans Hospital and Camp Murray, home of the Washington National Guard. On a clear day you can see all the way to the Capitol Building in Olympia, 25 miles to the south.

Finally, the east, a vista some might consider a combination of agony and ecstasy. There is some agonizing over the air pollution and industrial odors in the foreground (much has been done; much still needs to be done); there is also pride in the fact that the Port Industrial Area — the "Tideflats" to the natives — is truly alive with the sound of commerce. Beyond the industrial scene the fertile Puyallup Valley spreads on to the Cascade foothills, its once flourishing bulb and berry fields gradually giving way to creeping commercialism of a less attractive nature. Beyond the valley is the ecstasy, the snowy peaks of the Cascades, presided over by Mount Rainier, nee Mount Tacoma, "The Mountain That Was God."

Tacoma has a setting which is not easily improved upon — sheltered salt water to the north and west, fresh water lakes to the south, and snow-covered mountains to the east.

It is true that this fortuitous marriage of water, forests and mountains is not always in view. The postcard vistas occasionally are obscured by our famous rain. But when the scenery returns, it's always my favorite color, green.

If you prefer brown, go live in Los Angeles. Or Phoenix. Or El Paso.

Built to be a landmark, sumptuous hotel, Stadium High School is probably the only castle of learning in the nation. And definitely still a landmark.

Traffic on Union Avenue increases dramatically when the fall foliage season comes to the city.

There is probably no more photogenic community anywhere. So here's another look at Gig Harbor.

Truck farming is still an integral part of the rural charm on Tacoma's fringe. Early morning near the Puyallup River and the community of Fife.

One of the numerous elegant estates in the Lakes
district south of the city near Lakewood.

Overleaf: Steilacoom, oldest incorporated city in the
state, is a picturesque neighbor located a few miles
south of the Narrows Bridge.

Another Larry Anderson sculpture, in Wright Park;
cameo role by the photographer's son.

Overleaf: Traditional May Day celebration at
Tacoma's prestigious Annie Wright School in Old
Town.

Simple elegance of an older home, lovingly maintained, is a hallmark of Tacoma neighborhoods.

Spring, summer and fall, Tacoma homeowners can surround themselves with as much floral beauty as the green thumb can endure.

Lakewold, on the shore of American Lake, is part of the Corydon Wagner estate to be opened for public viewing.

The Neighborhoods

Ever since early residents of Old Tacoma grew up distrusting and competing with early residents of New Tacoma, the people who live and work in the area have had a strong sense of neighborhood. Meeting people after I arrived in Tacoma, fresh from the University of Washington, in the early 1950s, I was repeatedly asked where I'd gone to school. I quickly learned that nobody cared about my higher education at the "U-Dub;" indeed they wouldn't have been impressed with Harvard, or Oxford, or the Sorbonne.

They were waiting to hear "Stadium," or "Lincoln" or "Bellarmine." Or maybe even "Clover Park." If I'd been able to answer with one of the four, they would have started firing names and areas at me, emerging with a pretty good profile of the new kid. (They didn't know what to make of an outlander from Everett, although we did have some memorable Cross-State League football games to talk about.)

The importance of high school affiliation has been substantially diluted in subsequent years by the construction of a whole bunch of new ones, and by the Tacoma School Board's open enrollment policy. But one still gets assessed by his neighborhood. Tacoma's neighborhoods are many and diverse, and cataloguing them is no easy task for an outsider. Some are still anchored by high schools, others by colleges, junior highs, grade schools, parks or taverns. Taverns like the Titlow, the

Traditional neighborhood Americana.

Firwood, and Hank's at N. 6th and K come to mind. Sort of like neighborhood pubs.

A few ethnic neighborhoods survive, though in diluted form. You can still throw a rock in Old Town or Gig Harbor (though I wouldn't advise it) with a pretty good chance of hitting an "ich" — a person of Slav descent with a name like Petrich, or Stancich. But there have been a lot of changes. The Hilltop neighborhood above the central business district used to be primarily Scandinavian and Italian; now it's predominately black. And there's been a substantial Asian immigration, resulting in Korean, Vietnamese, Cambodian and Thai neighborhoods.

For me, the next best thing to growing up in Tacoma was being a newspaperman here for 35 years. I can discuss neighborhoods well enough to fool a few of the natives. Ohop or Oakland, Manitou or McKinley Hill, Day Island or Dash Point, Prospect Hill or Portland Avenue, Rosedale or Redondo, Salmon Beach or Summit View, I could get you there okay.

You could do a lot worse than settle down in one of them. Historian Murray Morgan cites the anonymous visitor to the Pacific Northwest quoted in an 1894 issue of *Harper's Weekly,* "Well, gentlemen, if I were a man of wealth seeking a home and investments on Puget Sound, I would live in Tacoma and invest in Seattle."

"He had it right," Murray added.

Gig Harbor. Instead of Mt. Rainier in the background, those are the Olympic Mountains not too distant from this nearby community, often affectionately referred to as Giggle Harbor.

Tacoma's nationally renowned Daffodil Parade is for everyone.

The People

A recent *TV Guide* listing, "Western Washington Edition" yet, referred to a program featuring "Seattle's Jeff Smith, the Frugal Gourmet." I winced slightly, since my friend Jeff lives two hills to my left, in Tacoma's North End. This frequently happens to Tacomans who achieve some celebrity — those writing about them either don't know where Tacoma is, or figure nobody else does. But my wince was slight — a product of mixed emotions. It's sort of like having your daughter selected as a *Playboy* centerfold: probably more exposure than we really need.

In truth, Tacoma gets a mention more often than not in pieces about its sons and daughters that have made good. Bing Crosby was born here, although he moved to Spokane with his family when he was 2. Others sent off to the show business wars include Bruce Bennett, an early Tarzan who was Herman Brix when he put the shot for Stadium High; Janis Paige, another Stadium product; Darren McGavin, who grew up in the suburban Dyslin Boys Ranch, an orphanage; and Dyan Cannon, who was Samille Diane Friesen when she went to Lowell School.

Students at University of Puget Sound enjoy a lazy spring day to study at The Fountain.

Some show business types have adopted Tacoma following their successes. Shirley MacLaine and her daughter have a home near Graham, toward The Mountain, where Shirley does much of her writing. Linda Evans has an estate on Gravelly Lake where she "gets away from it all." Yaphet Kotto lives with his family in the Tacoma suburbs, commuting to Hollywood for movie and television roles.

Olympic Gold Medalists from Tacoma have included Gretchen Kunigk Fraser, skiing; Kaye Hall, swimming; and Sugar Ray Seales and Davey Armstrong, boxing. Other world-class area athletes are Earl Anthony in bowling, Ron Cey in baseball and Lou Whittaker in mountaineering.

Besides the "Frugal Gourmet," Mr. Smith, a Methodist minister and once the chaplain at the University of Puget Sound, Tacoma is also the adopted home of the "Galloping Gourmet," Graham Kerr, now deeply involved in religious pursuits.

The state's current governor, Booth Gardner, is on loan from Tacoma, and two of his predecessors, Al Rosellini and Dixy Lee Ray, have Tacoma roots. Dixy now makes her home nearby on Fox Island. Tacoma's last U.S. Senator was the late Harry Cain, the focus of controversy during his post-World War II term.

In the world of commerce, Tacoma boasts of Henry Foss, whose mother, Thea, was the original "Tugboat Annie." George Weyerhaeuser has been president of the family "tree-growing company" for several decades. George Russell, Jr. parlayed an idea — the rating of money managers for corporate pension funds — into a multi-million dollar Tacoma-based business. A few years ago I was able to enumerate a dozen Tacomans who had been presidents of national business or professional organizations.

Tacoma has interesting people, talented people, friendly people, and caring people.

We did have the Guinness Book's world distance spitting champion, but I think he moved.

Overleaf: Although declining the past several years, the cut flower and bulb industry is significant to the Puyallup Valley, and the families who maintain the tradition.

Devotees of this age-old sport take advantage of the manicured bowling greens in the city's downtown Wright Park.

Thousands of runners participate in the annual
"Sound to Narrows" marathon, including major
contingents from nearby Fort Lewis and McChord AFB.

Overleaf: Old Town Dock on Ruston Way, at sunset.
Looking west to the Olympic Mountains.

The Water

There are those who turn up their noses at the mention of water. W.C. Fields comes to mind: "We lost our corkscrew and were forced to subsist for several days on food and water..." But most of us feel more kindly toward water. If not to drink, or be pelted with, at least to gaze at and frolic upon in its collected state.

If you are satisfied simply to look at it, Tacoma is tough to beat. Thousands of its homes have marine views, and public vantage points abound — along Ruston Way, on Five-Mile Drive — even Northeast Tacoma's Marine View Drive lives up to its name.

As a dedicated bay-watcher, I'm here to testify that it beats the heck out of daytime television. Great containerships and grain tankers arrive in Commencement Bay almost hourly from throughout the world, to be greeted by tire-wrapped tugboats. The ships of commerce share the water with the boats of pleasure. The little sailboats race each Saturday morning and Wednesday evening, and the larger sailboats, with their colorful spinnakers, are much in evidence on sunny weekends.

The lure of boat-ownership proves irresistible for many who settle here, although there's a gospel-like observation about boat-owners which refuses to die. His two happiest days, it is widely alleged, are the day he buys it, and the day he sells it.

If you want to get on the water without becoming a boat-owner, you still have lots of options. You can rent a small boat at the newly rebuilt Pont Defiance Boathouse, or charter a yacht at one of several marinas. The modern sightseeing boat, the Spirit of Tacoma, offers a variety of regularly scheduled cruises from its berth at The Dock, located appropriately enough, on Dock Street.

Then there are the ferries. The state ferry to Vashon Island leaves its Point Defiance slip for the trip hourly (with an exception or two) each day. The county operates a smaller ferry from Steilacoom to Ketron and Anderson islands. The county's smallest ferry (12 cars, if they're compacts) runs from Longbranch to Herron Island.

Harvesting a day's catch on Commencement Bay.

Despite the fact that Puget Sound water is frankly cold, a lot of people insist on immersing their bodies in it. Point Defiance's Owen Beach and Dash Point State Park are particularly popular local Sound spots on hot days. Warmer water can be found in the local public pools, and at public access beaches on American, Steilacoom, Wapato and Spanaway Lakes, as well as on smaller lakes in Eastern Pierce County. If you have little kids pleading to get wet, the painless answer involves visiting Federal Way's Enchanted Village, with its Wild Waves Park.

Yes, it's water, water everywhere, and you can even drink it without making a face. The tap water is imported from the Green River, and does well in taste-test contests. Try it with Scotch, W.C.

A labor of love, preparing for the annual Christmas Boat Parade along the shores of Commencement Bay is an annual treat for thousands of viewers.

Lake Steilacoom, one of the three lakes just south of Tacoma's city limits. Gravelly Lake and American Lake are the other two.

High tides and wind off the Tacoma Narrows can be an occasional nightmare, but residents of Day Island below University Place, consider their waterside living worth the threats.

Part of the Gig Harbor fishing fleet, on an early spring morning.

*Sunrise over one of the many pleasure boat marinas
on Commencement Bay.*

*Overleaf: One of the many parks in Tacoma's
metropolitan area, Wapato Park with its lake is
a joy to the city's southeast area residents.*

The Parks

O, give me a home where the buffalo roam? Dr. Brewster Higley wrote it. Dr. David Hellyer is living it. The Tacoma pediatrician and his wife, Connie, deeded a large tract of land near Eatonville to Tacoma's Park District which has become Northwest Trek, a wild animal park open to the public. The Hellyers retained their home on the park's small lake, and can watch through their living room windows as the bison, as well as the moose, elk, deer and other animals, quench their thirst.

Public parks abound in the Tacoma area. Two National Parks — Rainier and Olympic — are within view. Two state parks on Puget Sound — Dash Point to the north and Kopachuck to the west — are within 20 minutes of the city.

Jewel of the Tacoma park system is Point Defiance Park, 640 acres of onetime Indian Reservation land transferred to the city by the Territorial Legislature in 1888. Hare & Hare, father-and-son landscape architects from Kansas City, laid out the park in 1902, preserving the bulk of it in its natural state. It opened to the public in 1905, and now features a recently upgraded zoo where Pacific Rim animals are shown to advantage; an aquarium, a replica of Fort Nisqually and a logging camp, Camp Six, complete with an operating steam train; a storybook land for young children; and, on the water, Owen Beach and a new boathouse.

Near Commencement Park, in Old Town.

Wright Park, a 27-acre arboretum near downtown Tacoma, offers a Seymour Botanical Conservatory, large duck pond, bowling on the green and horseshoe pits. Its South End counterpart is Wapato Park, with a respectably sized lake and great picnic spots. Small parks abound throughout the city; my favorites include Firemen's Park, along downtown's A Street bluff, which boasts the onetime "World's Largest Totem Pole" and one of several Larry Anderson sculptures which grace local parks; and Commencement Park, adjacent to the Old Town Dock, where Schuster Parkway meets Ruston Way.

Pierce County has its own fine park system. Spanaway Park, adjacent to the Mountain Highway, offers the Spanaway Lake beaches, boathouse and picnic grounds, and the Sprinker Recreation Area next door. The county also has developed the former Western State Hospital dairy farm at Fort Steilacoom into a busy park, where Waughop Lake attracts catfish anglers and remote-control model boat enthusiasts.

Meanwhile, Tacoma's Ruston Way waterfront is being quietly acquired by the city and is well on its way toward becoming a scenic multi-mile park for walkers, joggers, bicyclists and boat-watchers.

If we had any more parks there wouldn't be room for all the branch banks and fast-food restaurants we need.

Mount Rainier National Park, where for decades photographers have found magnificent vistas for shooting "the mountain."

One of the reasons for "world class" recognition of the Point Defiance Zoo is the underwater viewing facility that attracts thousands of visitors annually.

Showtime for the spectators at Point Defiance Park's Rocky Shores exhibition center.

A photographer's dream, the Japanese Garden in Point Defiance Park.

Another jewel in the city's Wright Park, the Seymour Botanical Conservatory, a year 'round attraction.

Northwest Trek, near Eatonville southeast of Tacoma, is a natural habitat park featuring a growing number of wild animals indigenous to the Pacific Northwest.

Firemen's Park overlooks City Waterway, in downtown Tacoma.

Overleaf: Attendance at the Western Washington Fair in Puyallup now exceeds 1.1 million annually. Not only is it the largest single attraction held in the state, it's one of the 10 largest fairs in North America.

Having a Taste of Tacoma, thousands of eager-eaters take a sun break at this new, popular food fair held in Point Defiance Park.

The Action

There are those, notably Seattle snobs (possibly redundant), who would argue that "Tacoma" and "Action" are contradictions in terms.

Okay. To get to the "major league" action — the Seahawks, the Sonics, the Mariners, the Huskies, the Seattle Symphony and the opera — Tacomans need to drive north on the I-5 Freeway for 45 minutes.

But there are two flip sides to this unusually shaped coin. 1 — A Tacoman also needs to drive north for 45 minutes to find traffic congestion, parking problems and outrageous prices. And 2 — What action there is in Tacoma isn't all that shabby.

In fact, since the Tacoma Dome opened in 1983, a lot of Seattleites have been driving south for 45 minutes to see the likes of Frank Sinatra, Bruce Springsteen, Neil Diamond and Michael Jackson; as well as major sporting events like the National U.S. Figure Skating Championships and the NCAA Women's College Basketball Finals.

The Dome has been the home of the Tacoma Stars franchise in the Major Indoor Soccer League, where the locals have competed with teams from Chicago, Baltimore, Dallas, San Diego, Los Angeles and other metropolitan centers in the fast-paced, American version of the world's most popular sport.

And while baseball fans have to go indoors (and pay major league prices) to watch the Mariners in Seattle's Kingdome, the Tacoma Tigers (the Oakland A's triple-A affiliate) play the game as God intended, outdoors, on grass, in Cheney Stadium, one of the finest minor league ballparks in the nation.

Well-supported civic events include the Puyallup Valley Daffodil Festival in April with its Grand Floral Street Parade traversing Tacoma, Puyallup, Sumner and Orting on a Saturday, followed by decorated yachts in a marine parade along Ruston Way on the following Sunday.

Remember your first raw oyster?

The Western Washington Fair in Puyallup, which spans three September weekends, is the state's biggest. Its grandstand show includes a rodeo and headliners who've ranged from Bob Hope, Red Skelton and Willie Nelson to Alabama, the Oakridge Boys and the Flying Wallendas.

The Fourth of July fireworks show packs the Old Tacoma hillside, and is usually preceded by sailboat races and an air show. Downtown, there's an annual street fair and an annual bed race; and there are Christmas parades, both on the street and on the water.

Every day, of course, there are the magnificent parks, the viewpoints, and the wonderful people. A picnic is always possible. Just make sure everyone has an umbrella handy. And take along a portable radio to listen to the rush-hour traffic reports from Seattle.

The annual Daffodil Parade draws spectacular, flower bedecked floats from throughout the Northwest.

*The 4th of July fireworks display off Commencement
Park in Old Town equals any held in the nation.*

*Overleaf: Pierce County residents are rightfully proud
of the Tacoma Dome, which since its completion in
1984 has won national acclaim for its sports,
entertainment and convention facilities.*

The Stars these exhuberant fans are exhorting are the Tacoma team of the national Major Indoor Soccer League.

The Stars in action in the Dome, playing before a typically large crowd and the once highly controversial Antonakos neon sculpture.

Acknowledged as one of the finest minor league baseball parks in America, Cheney Field is home to the Tacoma Tigers of the AAA Pacific Coast League.

Tacoma Country & Golf Club, founded in 1894, is one of the premier golf courses in the Pacific Northwest and one of three private courses in the area. There are numerous public courses, also.

The Woodbrook Hunt Club rides to the hounds virtually the year 'round, on the prairies of the sprawling Fort Lewis reservation, south of the city.

Off Pt. Defiance, these anglers are in pleasant pursuit of the fighting King or Silver salmon.

Overleaf: Just as church towers seem to dominate the landscapes of much of New England, so do they enrich Tacoma's scenery. Visitation Catholic Church, in South Tacoma.

The Temples

Some local philosophers' — most of whom hold court on downtown bar stools — contend that one of Tacoma's major problems stems from the fact that the city never had a major turn-of-the-century fire, like Seattle and San Francisco did.

"They sure got rid of a lot of junk that way," one latter-day Socrates told me. "In Tacoma, we've just had to sit here and watch some parts of the city decay."

There is some truth in the observation. Tacoma has been plagued by selective fires — many of which have wiped out Tacoma treasures. We mourn the passing of the elegant, Stanford White-designed Tacoma Hotel, which opened on the A Street bluff in 1884 and set the social standard for the Pacific Northwest until it burned in 1935. The imposing brick Tacoma Theater Building at 9th and Broadway, which housed the Music Box, went up in flames in 1963. My favorite bar, located in the boat-shaped Top of the Ocean Restaurant in

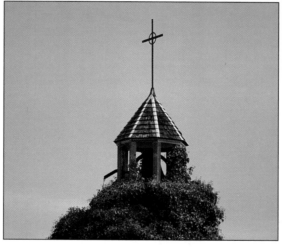

The bell tower of St. Peter's Episcopal in Old Town, the city's first church, built in 1873.

Old Town, became history when it was torched by an arsonist during the county's "Bar Wars" in the '70s.

But some good buildings have survived and some have been added. Tacoma has its temples.

A financial panic and a fire figured in the ultimate opening of Stadium High School, quite possibly the most spectacular high school in the nation. The Northern Pacific Railroad began building it in the early 1890s as a luxury hotel — supposedly an exact copy of a French castle. Construction stopped when the NP went bankrupt in the Panic of 1893,

and the partially finished hotel was damaged by fire in 1898. The remains were taken over by the Tacoma School Board, the original hotel design was adapted to that of a high school by architect Fred Heath, and Stadium opened as Tacoma High School in 1906. The Tacoma Stadium, now known as Stadium Bowl, was built in the adjacent gulch a few years later.

Tacoma's massive, domed Union Station was bustling from 1911 to 1925 and still stands, though damaged by earthquakes and abandoned by Amtrak. Restoration efforts center around a move of the Washington State Historical Society and the need for a federal courts facility.

St. Peter's Church in Old Town dates from 1873; Sunday evening prayer services still are held. St. Luke's Episcopal Church, built in 1882 at 6th and Broadway, was moved stone by stone and rebuilt in the '40s at North 36th and Gove. If you like steeples, Holy Rosary's landmark spire rose at the end of South Tacoma Avenue in 1920-21; while the North End answered with the impressive First Presbyterian Church tower at Tacoma and Division Avenues.

Tacoma's skyline changed dramatically in the '80s with the addition of the award-winning Sheraton Hotel at 13th and Broadway, the Finanacial Center Building across the street, and the new Frank Russell Building on A Street, adjacent to the old Tacoma Hotel site, now Firemen's Park.

Tacoma finally is in respectable architectural shape. Cancel the fire.

Built in 1921, Holy Rosary Church's splendid spire has been a familiar Tacoma landmark for north and south-bound motorists, on Old Highway 99 and today's Interstate 5.

*A classic landmark at the corner of Division and
Tacoma Avenues — First Presbyterian Church.*

*Getting the vocal chords warmed up before services at
the African Methodist Episcopal Church in the city's
south end.*

*Overleaf: The Science Building at University of Puget
Sound, in the city's north end. A nationally acclaimed
School of Law is located in downtown Tacoma.*

The Culture

Let's admit it right up front: Tacoma is not the Glory-That-Was-Rome Revisited. Tacoma has long been your basic blue-collar, working man's town. When a hue and cry was raised over the city's expenditure of $280,000 for Antonakos' neon squiggles to satisfy the requirement for public art in the Tacoma Dome, some Seattle art critics called us Philistines. Maybe a lot of us are. But few of us travel to Seattle on turnip trucks. This city has a healthy appreciation for the so-called Finer Things in Life.

One reason most Tacomans will feel comfortable in the 21st Century is the existence of our two fine, long-established private universities. Both the University of Puget Sound, which celebrated its Centennial in 1987, and Pacific Lutheran University, in suburban Parkland, boast respected departments of music, art and drama. Their efforts to keep the community culturally awake have been aug-

The campus at Pacific Lutheran University, renowned for its liberal arts curriculum, especially music, and recent national championship sports teams.

mented in recent years by those of Tacoma Community College, in the city's West End, and Pierce College, in the Fort Steilacoom area.

There are indications that the missionary work by the disciples of higher education has paid off. In the early '80s, public and private subscriptions paid for the restoration of the once and currently elegant Pantages Theatre at 9th and Broadway. Now a sparkling showcase for musical and dramatic presentations, as well as classic films, the Pantages has been a large part of the rebirth of Tacoma's civic pride.

The Tacoma Actors Guild provides continu-

ing seasons of professional dramatic productions, while published amateur plays are offered by the Tacoma Little Theater, Lakewood Players, and other community theatrical groups.

Support for the Tacoma Symphony Orchestra and its longtime conductor, Edward Seferian, has been so strong the orchestra is able to perform a number of free public concerts each year, many with distinguished guest soloists.

Jan Collum, who presides over Balletacoma, and Jo Emery, founder and artistic director of the Tacoma Performing Dance Co., have launched professional careers for dozens of local dancers.

The Tacoma Art Museum, located in the onetime Bank of Washington Building at 12th and Pacific, has been the recipient of several valuable permanent collections, and always features a popular children's exhibit.

Our area boasts several sculptors whose work is recognized and praised beyond the city limits. Larry Anderson's moving, lifelike bronzes have added considerable class to Tacoma's parks — and sidewalks, even.

The list of Tacoma's published authors and poets, its successful painters and designers, is much too long to be included here. But they are definitely out there.

And the neon art still lights up the Dome, the original outcry having quieted to a murmur. At that, it's probably better than Andy Warhol's proposed giant rooftop flower.

Home of Tacoma's highly successful "Balletacoma" Dance Company is the Jan Collum School of Classical Ballet, an institution of the city's arts community.

A major symbol of Tacoma's rebirth of civic pride was the restoration of the historic Pantages Theater to its original elegance in the early 1980's. Outside, and inside (opposite).

The Rialto Theatre, its very name symbolic of the early days of motion pictures, is still in business off Broadway, at Ninth.

Eastvold Auditorium at Pacific Lutheran University, performance center for the school's superb musical and theatrical productions.

Overleaf: The booming Industrial Tideflats, home of the mercurial Port of Tacoma with a rapidly growing, international reputation as a containership, import and export facility.

The Providers

Should some despot build a Berlin-type Wall around the Tacoma area, at least the inmates would be able to eat pretty well.

A lot of good things to eat are made or processed, and canned or packaged, in Tacoma. And here is a reassuring insight from one who has hung around town for a spell: I have frequently seen these products eaten by people who work where they are made! A partial menu:

The output of Hygrade's Tacoma plant has pretty much been reduced to Ball Park Franks, but they make as fine a hot dog as you'll find. (They plump, you know.)

The suburban Pederson Fryer Farms boast one of the state's largest chicken-producing facilities.

Fine flavors still grow in Tacoma's Nalley Valley, where Nalley's Foods turns out many varieties of chili, potato chips, pickles and other food items.

For dessert, we can always count on the Brown & Haley Candy Co., which

Early morning beauty "a-mist" the steamy plumes above the Industrial Tideflats.

sends Almond Roca to a number of foreign countries, sells lots of Mountain Bars and features many other confections on its ever-changing production lines.

There are all kinds of fish lurking beneath the surrounding salt water, and if you can't manage to consume it fresh from one of our several fish markets, you can buy your salmon kippered or smoked, and get your clams, geoducks and oysters in cans.

For a quick lunch, it's hard to beat Adams Peanut Butter on Roman Meal Bread — both Tacoma products. And Johnny's Seasoning Salts are sold throughout the West.

Tacoma also turns out the grocery bags to hold these products. The landmark pulp mill and bag plant long operated by St. Regis, then Champion, is now a Simpson company.

Copper is no longer smelted here; the Tacoma Smelter stands idle, a victim of dwindling markets and environmental concerns. Boat-building isn't what it once was, but it still happens.

The lumber mills which used to line the waterfront are pretty much gone. The log trucks still roll into the industrial tideflats, but the logs now are primarily an export commodity and are sawed up elsewhere, usually in Japan.

The Port of Tacoma has achieved its early major league promise and is a blockbuster industry in itself. The Port is a major import center for foreign cars. Containerships parade in and out of Commencement Bay with all manner of cargoes. Grain tankers line up at Tacoma's modern grain terminal to carry midwestern grain to foreign ports across the Pacific. Freight trains and semi-trucks radiate out from the Port yards 24 hours a day.

While local heavy industry has declined, some small entrepreneurs are getting bigger. A generation of Western kids are growing with playground equipment put together by Tacoma's BigToys Co. And a young Tacoman has had some success making, packaging and selling skipping rocks. Mother Nature needs a little competition to keep her on her toes.

Cargo-handling facilities in Tacoma's port are considered among the finest on the West Coast.

Millions of board feet of raw timber are exported from Tacoma to Pacific Rim countries.

*Coming through the city's port facilities are
thousands of foreign-made automobiles.*

Hard work, even on a calm morning, but commercial fishing is still a viable industry in much of Puget Sound, including Commencement Bay.

One of the city's two high-speed, powerful hovercraft fireboats makes one of its many daily equipment checks, just inside the City Waterway.

Overleaf: McChord AFB is home for giant C-141B Starlifters (pictured here), C-130 Hercules and F-15 Eagle fighter-interceptors.

The Army's Fort Lewis, immediately south of McChord AFB, covers 70,000 acres donated by the city in 1917.

The Protectors

The Tacoma area's lengthy co-existence with the military has, for the most part been a comfortable one.

During the Great War and for a time thereafter, military commanders complained about the city and county's apparent tolerance of prostitution, frequently slapping "Off Limits" designations on local areas and establishments.

And the natives still complain from time to time about jet noise and sonic booms, artillery practice and wayward soldiers and airmen.

But the military's public relations have been good. Fort Lewis provides Tacoma with its civic Christmas tree, McChord gives invaluable air-sea rescue support, and both bases come up with bands for parades and concerts and generals for civic committees.

The biggest plus is the economic impact. The military provides thousands of civilian jobs and a big influx of money for local merchants and suppliers.

Fort Lewis, home of the 9th Infantry Division, is a sprawling installation south of the city. It dates from 1917 when Tacoma and Pierce County residents, at the urging of Frank. S. Baker, then publisher of The Tribune, and a couple other civic leaders, voted overwhelmingly to issue bonds of up to $2 million to purchase 70,000 acres and donate it to the federal government for such a facility.

This was in January. Congress declared war on Germany that April, by late August construction was under way, and by December some 40,000 young men were training at the Army camp, named for explorer Meriwether Lewis.

Among the celebrated military leaders who have passed through its portals was Dwight Eisenhower. He was assigned to Fort Lewis in 1939, while a lieutenant colonel. He saw his son, John, graduate from Stadium High School;

Our No. 2 state flower — Scotchbroom.

in 1941 Ike was promoted to colonel and was transferred to a new command in Texas. His subsequent rise has been well documented.

McChord Air Force Base, originally Pierce County Airport and later Tacoma Municipal Airport, was turned over to the federal government in 1938 and named for Col. William A. McChord, a distinguished Army Air Corps flyer who'd been killed in a crash the previous year.

McChord began as a dirt strip with a single hangar and several biplanes. With the rumblings in Europe came B-18 and B-23 bombers. McChord became the country's largest bomber training base during World War II, the primary aircraft being the B-25 Mitchell medium bomber.

The 4,500-acre base currently is home to the Military Airlift Command's 25th Air Division, flying C-141B Starlifters and the C-130 Hercules; the Tactical Air Command's 25th Air Division and the 318th Fighter Interceptor Squadron, flying the F-15 Eagle.

McChord also hosts the Air Force Reserve's 446th Military Airlift Wing, with a complement of 2,600 men and women from Washington, Oregon, Idaho, Utah and Colorado.

Other military installations south of Tacoma include the Madigan Army Hospital complex, the American Lake Veterans Hospital; Camp Murray, home of the Washington National Guard; and North Fort Lewis, used primarily as a training ground for national guardsmen from other states.

A Naval Reserve destroyer unit, Coast Guard patrol boat unit and a National Guard waterborne unit are located on Commencement Bay. Nearby Bremerton is home of the massive Puget Sound Naval Shipyard, temporary home for the Navy's largest ships of the line.

Overleaf: You'll find Alder Lake on the way to Mount Rainier. Its serenity just might make the trip a little longer.

The Mood

The Tacoma area's mood is definitely upbeat as the state celebrates its '89 Centennial. Part of the reason has to do with chips.

Not the mountains of wood chips on the Simpson Company's tideflats property, waiting to become paper bags.

And not the endless river of potato chips flowing from the Nalley's plant in Nalley Valley.

But the chips which reside on the shoulders of several generations of Tacomans as the city gradually lost its battle for supremacy on the Sound to Seattle.

Tacoma and Seattle began the 20th Century nearly even and the rivalry was intense. Tacoma's hatred for Seattle grew white-hot as Seattle repeatedly rebuffed efforts to have "Tacoma," a form of which most Indians had called The Mountain, supplant the name Captain Vancouver had bestowed to honor his friend, British Adm. Peter Rainier.

The wounds have mostly healed. The old timers are pretty much gone, the hatred with them. The chips have fallen where they may.

Tacoma residents accept the fact that their city is Number Two on the Sound, and they've found that the slower lane has its advantages. Homes are cheaper. Traffic and parks are less congested. There is a greater sense of community.

And when there's a major league game or a major league concert, opera or ballet to see in the Big City, it's just 45 minutes away on Interstate 5. Tacomans no longer need apologize for most of the negative city aspects Seattleites loved to joke about.

The once-shabby central business district is a treat to visit. The skyline, which not too long ago consisted almost entirely of a neon, flying-red horse atop the Washington Building, finally makes Tacoma look like a city.

The knowledge that the quality is there and respectability has been achieved has made it easier for Tacomans to accept and appreciate the funkier aspects of their environment.

It's possible to applaud a prima ballerina in the Pantages one night and play pool in a tavern shaped like a coffee pot (Bob's Java Jive) the next. Or visit the gorilla and play baseball with a chicken at the B & I Circus Store. Or applaud Art's Hamburgers' one-man sidewalk landscaping effort on Pacific Avenue.

And where else can you go to high school in a castle?

Most Tacoma faces these days convey a relaxed confidence.

Millionaires and bums nod to each other as they stroll and walk their dogs along the public concourse on the Ruston Way waterfront. (Do not, however, try to read anything on the faces of the joggers; joggers in any city appear to be unhappy as hell.)

But take away the faces of the joggers, of the drivers caught in traffic jams headed for a Dome concert, and the basic mood is laid-back assurance.

When Gov. Booth Gardner's driver stops at Frisko Freeze on Division Avenue and picks up a couple of doubleburgers for the gov — toiling at his desk in the back of the van — it's no big deal.

When Frugal Gourmet Jeff Smith grabs lunch at Honan's downtown Irish saloon, home of the "chef du jour," and cleans his plate, it's no big deal.

When Linda Evans, in bandana and dark glasses, goes shopping in a Lakewood supermarket, it's no big deal.

It's not the fast lane, but it's not exactly the slow lane, either. It may be the best of all possible lanes.

Hey, all this and Indian bingo, every night.

Tranquility is synonymous with familiar Tacoma area waterscapes like this one.

An exciting example of neighborhood rennaissance.
You'll find these renewed Victorian houses on J Street.

Autumn mood; early morning in the Puyallup Valley near Sumner.

The Future

"It is bad enough to know the past," W. Somerset Maugham is said to have said. "It would be intolerable to know the future."

Unless, of course, you happen to be a horseplayer.

The future remains a mystery, Somerset would doubtless be happy to know, despite an occasional lucky prediction by a supermarket tabloid psychic.

There are signs, however. Omens, portents, trends.

In Tacoma's case, most of the signs seem to be promising. After all, Tacoma was blessed from the beginning with a magnificent setting. Heaven and nature sang when Tacoma was created. The climate, on the moist side, is generally agreed to be salubrious — a 50-cent word meaning pleasant — when compared to most other locales.

The old and the new, early 1900's (presently the Pierce County Medical Building) and mid-1980's (Tacoma Sheraton Hotel).

For more than 100 years a lot of folk have done their best to screw up that which heaven and nature bestowed, but heaven and nature have managed to attract quite a few disciples, and the good guys seem finally to have the upper hand.

Tacoma is bruised and a bit bloody, but Tacoma is a survivor.

Tacoma has survived severe economic reversals, flagrant political scandals and the best shots of Seattle's editorial writers and stand-up comics.

Tacoma has survived the loss of a great many jobs in the lumber and plywood mills, boatbuilding plants and the copper smelter.

Tacoma's downtown has survived a long period of absentee ownership and the body blow it received with the opening of the Tacoma Mall.

Through the worst of times, Tacoma held onto and protected its great parks. Point Defiance, considered by many the finest park in the Pacific Northwest, now boasts a world-class zoo.

The city has quietly bought up much of the available Ruston Way waterfront, and it has become a focal point for the city's outdoor activity.

As was pointed out in earlier chapters, the Port of Tacoma is on a roll, food-processing remains a major industry, and the area gained a taste of high-tech when the Fairchild Corporation built a semiconductor plant on Puyallup's South Hill.

An outward and visible sign of the city's promising future is the handsome new Frank Russell Building, on downtown's A Street bluff, overlooking the bay. The building is a tribute to Tacoma and a monument to an idea conceived by the company's president and major stockholder, George Russell.

It occurred to George that large corporations, with billions of dollars in pension funds to invest, needed guidance in selecting investment firms with which to entrust such serious money.

Thus was born a system which analyzes and rates money managers for the large corporations who need them.

Despite pressure from some clients to move his head office to a financial center like San Francisco or New York, George and wife Jane have decided they'd just as soon hang around Tacoma, thanks anyway.

With shrewd people like George Russell willing to invest in Tacoma, its future has to be better than promising.

Through all the turmoil and setbacks, Tacoma's major symbol of stability has been The Mountain. If you can't see The Mountain, it's raining. If you can see The Mountain, it's going to rain.

As they say, you can take it to the bank.

St. Joseph Hospital's main building is reflected in the downtown glass facade of a U S West Communications building.

Overleaf: She fell down once, was rebuilt, and stands today as Tacoma's signature of resiliency and strengths, essential qualities of a City of Destiny.